*Century Swept Brutal*

also by Zach Savich
*Full Catastrophe Living* (2009)
*Annulments* (2010)
*The Firestorm* (2011)
*Events Film Cannot Withstand* (2011)

Century Swept Brutal
by Zach Savich

**Black Ocean**
Boston · New York · Chicago

Black Ocean
P.O. Box 52030
Boston, MA 02205
blackocean.org

ISBN 978-1-939568-05-2


Library of Congress Cataloging-in-Publication Data

Savich, Zach.
  [Poems. Selections]
  Century Swept Brutal / Zach Savich.
    pages cm
  ISBN 978-1-939568-05-2 (alk. paper)
  I. Title.
  PS3619.A858A6 2014
  811'.6~dc23

                          2014000516


FIRST EDITION

# Contents

*for David Bartone*

*Century Swept Brutal*

*One*

I've tuned the piano so a certain chord

is always nearly happening.


As grasses thresh

against themselves, seeding

this field thicker

long before the farmer

turns atop

ladder fixed to the house by a gaze of ivy

The first lightning was

horizontal.

Sun

and skin

do not rhyme—

they are the same word. You can do anything

until it becomes beautiful

Acres of native glass. Trampolinists

in the square,

and the mechanic's

a florist now,

too. What I don't know

couldn't fill a book.


I stand under neon blazing between *hot* and *dog*

The presence of this

ingredient activates

surrounding flavors.

I don't know what

couldn't fill a book.

Time to throw in the match.

Watched a man

shoulder a mattress

shadows fell from.

This menu hardly mentions

the camellias.

I'm faking a fever

so you can touch me

Then one day

you see a street you know

in a novel. The hour turns

first inside

itself, she applies

lipstick to her reflection

in the cigarette

machine. I sing what any snapped string does. Taxis

slowing for an ambulance outside the cafe

called Florist. You can live like this, for a while,

remembering until some

appetite seizes, and you attend it, or don't

Asters in the sill

hat brim thin.

Willow's the only green for a time.

I place in a small envelope.

I gauge the season by what is in my hands

Green splints.

Sun chapped

so the mortar too is light.

Love will

or wills.

Inscribes a year in the first and now only brick.

In jeans with nothing in the pockets

In the park across the street

a boy rushes

from limit into limit

a kite of cardboard and

twined. I tell him the snake is air if you step on it.

I tell him the elephant's tusk extends all the way up

its face to the eye, it is an optic

nerve-tooth. And when fireflies rise like a revival tent,

bright and staked to nothing, he doesn't

call it a consolation for his verifiable powerlessness

but a further cause

Beauty being cause,

not effect; not perceived,

perceived with.


Century-swept, brutal, the new flags

dry on their wires.


It has taken me several years to note the fire-escape built
with a now-rusted roof so when it is raining or there is a
hose raining you will not be touched in descent

Say the heart's an antique

haydoor,

opening over nothing.


Stenciled lilies lend us local color,

over the sour money

of plucked

piñata clouds vivid in a ditch.


Asters snags.


Or soon enough

Having catalogued many things I am not surprised to see
the bird that each morning wakes me will one morning
lead me into death, it is startlingly ordinary that there
should not be separate angels but these two notes coming
to mean any message in turn, as apples heating in a shape
or a horse

The closest one gets to preferences is hours in a day.


The land was never

lyrical, we built

and birds

never named but personally (Glenda's

Singer, Mailbox Flag,

Stump

Cuckold, Shadow of the Ditch)

seem

merely aspects of vision or the continuous and still

uncoined air

*Two*

He said *When I say what I mean it sounds like a line* She said

*There's a way to look at the space between leaves*

*so when the leaves move these spaces*

*stay as they are* He said *I know what you*

*remind me of but not what for*

She said *The trees have gone past blossoming,*

*straight into green, I stand with a cookbook bound*

*in a plaid skirt, field floral from the odor*

*of dying grasses*

She said *In a country in rain*

*I entered the church with the others, a church*

*what we enter in rain, here the large*

*shopmart with trees inside*

*becoming open air again, the people*

*would've been here already* He said

*In which I carried you and*

*when you grew too heavy to carry I*

*carried you through the shallows of the bay*

He said *The grasses are dying from the wetness*

*this spring, which is also fertile, you have strung yarn*

*through the branches, I garden*

*with a glove with barbed wire inside* She said *As trees*

*coaxed to fruit in bottles, bangled*

*on their limbs and let rot unto ferment, I saw*

*the cozened plank over two furrows, tried to distinguish*

*between eros and art, mostly felt I should*

He said *So a radio doesn't*

*wear out the signal, we are wettest not*

*from the rain but the dripping*

*of leaves* She said *A girl came to my door*

*to return a nickel she found*

*on the path, I was laboring with*

*a project of robbing McDonald's*

*wearing for a mask a bag*

*I got from another McDonald's, eyes*

*green as antihistamines in a pond*

She said *I proposed to travel*

*asking anyone what's the most beautiful*

*thing you have seen*

*then I'd go to it and the route*

*would take me south, I remember*

*water tanks over*

*the hospital grounds with axes*

*to topple them and flood*

*the hospital grounds when there is a fire,*

*I held the kettle at a boil, Of memory as current*

*perception not nostalgia*

*each blow recalled all others*

*and softened them, so I took them in*

He said *The dying dog could barely walk but lunged*

*like nothing had happened,* We discussed

unknown reserves vs. new

energy generated by expending, How a lyric

sense changes as our minds/bodies do, We learn

by is it the rain or grasses racing today

parallel to my hand She said *The tall green overtook*

*the road,* while they said clarity and meant

we do not wish to see

we never have

She said *The open air grown labyrinthine*

*if I exit from this side gate,*

*leftover containers and gulls,*

*overall clouds*

*There could've been an ocean anywhere, that's*

*the kind of weathered*

*these hours are* He said *And the motions*

*in the heads of small birds*

*not looking or to hunt but*

*architectural*

He said *See the red raspberries straining* She said *No*

*the green cellular ones strained within, Now lift your arms*

*and hands remain down, Now in the dressmaker's window*

*the reflection of a street crosses a gown*

He said *See the red raspberries strained against*

*this wire that you could say educates them away from*

*the path but from which they rise*

*so haphazardly, it must be by design*

She said *They hose lemons from the highest branches,*

*run-off obsessing the bay*

He said *If in any age*

*you say we may share this bed but only*

*touch in these three places, which of course*

*in its restraint conjures*

*increased lust before we have finished imagining*

*restraint, and a tone*

*induces the shape of a bell, so the nets*

*drying in trees*

*occasionally have olives in them in the morning*

She said *The sheets literate, in the street*

*breezes correct for us, We move preceded by a vowel*

*Three*

There is a way to say it that doesn't remember

yet sees now because of / the epic

began at its core / inset: warrior dismantles

the messenger and builds

a gun from the severed wing / you asked me to drop

an orange / asked me to tear at

Consider instead the "impossibly beautiful" /

the painter regresses

unable to paint, he paints what he could

at other ages, craft transmitting

silence not heroic / most of what I read I can skim

recalling things I have written

A book wrapped in a towel / I followed

the ideas but they were far

from any lack I had / I wanted to be returned instead

to semblance, like a town I saw at seven *corrugate* /

humid day now words sunk in sky particulate

as pills in an opaque vial, and imagining's harder

"Daily or true" / I have met

a disgraced physician who will do

whatever he wants to you

for a reasonable cost / today so many

carrying gas cans / have you seen

my new eye whites tattoo?

Low clouds stained a pre-

tornado green among winged

things zinging among

sweetnesses, thick as sidewalk chalk stalks /

the one called Serenity has an arrow

in his brow / "palliative conditioning"

Mourning doves flake between

clothesline and roof / Confederate

patch tassels / each of my pleasures

is one of my only pleasures / it's not so bad

if you don't have a choice /

all problems only probabilities

Then what we'd called defiance we learned

to call grace / today I saw

flags blown so their thinnest

edges angled at me, nearly unseen /

obscure, but that's so we can touch / right

in the million-dollar slogan

Tapestry showed

mirror hung

on the frontmost ox's brow

as it drove

interlopers from a grove / each bale

a frozen trumpet at its core

Tapestry showed

red lines meaning we are

behind the eyes /

a shadow not attached to any tree /

not to any tree

visible through the birdsong

Tapestry showed

they dressed the nuns

had them waltz

with officers taking turns

reading sheet music stitched

into one another's backs

Tapestry showed

a hive

D's garden was

lilacs and

enough air

dusk in its white gloves

Waited out rain in the ostrich part /

have you seen my new eye whites tattoo? /

no one pulls down their pants

except to compare scars / you call that

a scar? / a crate stuffed with old calendars /

fake blood made of real saliva

*Four*

I had seen her many times

By the lake, which was a metal I didn't know about

That she fixed strawberries to the surface of

I saw her when wind lifted my laundry

From my window facing the water

The water had been made to look like another liquid

The consolation of everything still happening

Augmented by what her plain sitting proposed

I had seen that many times

Past an occasional chainsaw

Past my maps of deepnesses taped to the wall

As usual, I wanted to see the water and sky as separate
    forms of I don't know what

And name the clouds so they happened appropriately on
the tongue

And felt to do so was the World

This has been my primary employment since I can remember

Its satisfactions, and small rewards, come as the relaxed
manner one moves through heat with

I am not sure if the ground is under me now, having
walked on it already

I will never feel good in my body again

That day, I prepared a mug of tomato soup

The window's thickness was also part of the air

It was cloudy enough, I didn't need my glasses

But I assume it was warm in the sun

I assume yellow perch travel fastest when they are farthest
from our lines

I assume the sun releases minerals at depths its heat does
    not consider

She couldn't have wanted to read any book

Though two or three were beside her

I assume anything I say expresses the pain of my body

That the air in a tire looks like the weather here

That we are casual because dumbfounded

In spite of having spoken and imagined anything could
    change

The heat does not change, we dress for it

And if the lighthouse is underwater

The character has not been named in so long, he could be
    anyone

*Five*

1.

If you find our country's
real name
from you as ants
from the rinsed
wine bottle
precise as pop music
on the patio
of the concrete
biker bar
I wouldn't say
anybody'd pay you
the font
slashed at
makes America
look like the ocelot
on our ration
tickets you can exchange for
two teddies
a bud

2.

This is the look
of those hiding out
learned
to play the guitar
with his other hand
so no one'd
recognize
he knows only
one song
at a time
figures the chords
of what he doesn't
and somehow
the words will be revealed

3.

The waitress has
her own apartment
behind
the whole town
she can make
anything
into your choice
a mirror
or a lamp
I don't tell her
that's a reference
but am pleased to say
the only difference
is for a lamp
you need somewhere
for the wire

4.

I find I can imagine
her face best
when I see it
little chainsaws
burrowing
over her eyes
she keeps her supplies
in t-shirts
under driftwood
in a tub
she promises
to wash the smoke
from me in
in the morning

5.

The morning retains
with insects
under a rowboat propped
upside-down
near a vacant
field
still months from auction
I don't
need to remember
a scar on her
like filtrated
glass
nap here
no one
stencil on
the dragonfly
lips

6.

Our country doesn't have
enough evidence
to be held on
or for the boardwalk cops
with firework
mustaches
to care about
my fame
its secret handshake
is easy
involving pity
and a huge sun badge
on a blue
sideswipe
the police and me
shy from
whose van do you think
this is
with the goofy heavens
airbrushed on it
they photograph me against
for documentation

7.

About paradise
a man's muscles
I mean
motives
couldn't matter
gumminess
at the base of the eye
of a turtle
she fixed a lightbulb
to the throat of
oh I have
taken it out
alone with three oars
the noon's canoe is spacious
but looks like mine
I'll tell anyone who hails us
the creature isn't real

8.

At the idiots' convention
the only
thing no one collects
is himself
breakfast and
cocktails or
breakfast cocktails
their ties have rulers on them
so you know
here's where to cut
I must look like those recalled
tires
I have forgotten
I am looking for the next defensible
name of America
hay bales of hashbrowns
precision only
in a ketchup nozzle
that's so
like us

9.

Some proposed
names are easy
I get them
at bus stops
A Kind of Dying No One's Heard About
What We Thought
We Were Watching
Distances You Can Fall From
One Could Still Befriend Sculptors
Unharvestable Flowers

10.

By the time
anyone realized
this was
a town
most of the people had gone
to the big faux
antique shooting gallery
fake bears
real guns
in the earth
we found ourselves
with our most beautiful friend
wouldn't you like some advice

11.

The tire-
flat gull teaches more
about flying its bones
see hunger
is a wider body
one is a wind-
chime in
The mind is heat not
light
a light-
bulb in
the blackest pan
Love judges
water's depth not
by its darkness
A boulder purples
in the shade of an ant
The first
forgiveness is
the judgment of lust

(I keep
my hand in
my
pocket because my
finger is stuck
in a tiny
priceless vase)

12.

Light trims
the first waves OK
first because
wind now scarves
toward a cracker of beach
where I can't tell
the page number from
the time it is
the time
it *is* is when the hour
changes
only the colors on a page
and sometimes me
e.g. my relationship
to sorrow but not
my watch
it will be evening in my book
before anybody
out here
has seen if they have
enough foil
should we put this golden
lunar wine

in the ice hole?
I do not answer the call
from my dentist
my book contains the collected
poems of that other body of water
James Wright

*Six*

In the end is a blue I will describe only as white

I feel like I'm at the end of my rope

Think how the rope feels

When I was outlawed from writing poetry

Yet promised all the beer I could care about

I still took my shirt off only at dusk

When the lake got enameled by light and its benign cover-ups

Light I read where it fell

And I stood with the air carved out around me

Or at times caving in because of me

And I stood like an ancient wick

Light falling between the stories of my newspaper

I wrote this first in an impressive manner

With dragonflies

And she would please me by saying things like *I just now saw*

She said during the revolution portraits burned fastest

No one could paint them fast enough

Or sometimes two geese with four little geese between them

Swam near enough to see

An ancient wick is made of names too compressed to speak of

It should be darker than the night around it

Like berries sprained on a loose stone wall

And she'd return in her little boat

To a house with windows coiled pure as concertinas

The lake was green enough, you could pull a green bottle
  from it like it was nothing

And the man who came with my crate of beer each night

And left it in water that could be blue or green or white
or a loose stone wall

Hardly cared anymore if I had written

His daughter was still in the other country

In heat you don't move through, it's what moves

She was writing a novel about trying to hide the first buds
of the saplings

I know what I'm outlawed from saying

I showed him some screensavers I was working on

I showed him a new way I had invented for knotting my tie

*Seven*

He said *I see the glossy steps*

*of the silver ladder*

*touched by fallen*

*paint, glossy where that paint*

*has been scuffed away*

*by shoes soft as wolf-hair brushes*

She said *Now I can't tell*

*the idling motor*

*of my brother's car empty*

*in the garage*

*from the fire-escape perfectly along*

*every normal*

*staircase, The loon shoots up*

*the shadow*

*of the moon in translation*

He said *Then the bottoms*

*of my shoes wore*

*away, My teeth grew*

*into cubes of coconut jelly,*

*the blood*

*in my eyes congealed*

*into what I now have for pupils*

She said *But the mind is still*

*an abandoned*

*brewery you can kick*

*through the plywood and ascend*

*sawdust*

*and dead birds surround*

*absent kettles, Everything in there*

*is larger than a man, In spring*

*a helicopter*

*drops a thousand toy duckies, raffle*

*numbers dark on their breasts,*

*see mine*

He said *I can't tell*

*muscles from sun, sand*

*between the bare*

*grass rising with sun*

*to scrim the windows*

*from the lisp*

*of my hand against a bell*

*at the desk I stand at ringing*

*for myself*

She said *You make enough*

*each day*

*to pay for a night and Sunday*

*walk past the on-ramp*

*to the Mexican diner, My dress*

*is a lampshade*

*of skin with little green triangles*

*I have drawn on myself*

*for trees*

*Eight*

Day ages instantly, orange cones
at the corners of its eyes
you need to get out and pull
from the road. Whoever's
driving is my wife. Curdling shadows
of wires thick enough
to bump a pick-up. Some people
have to always go back
to see if it was a body. I'm like that
with clouds.

\*

Scree comes straight up
to the screen. I chip a brick
from the foundation
to prop the window with.
A traveling troupe
sets up on the stone path.
The whole yard is stone.
I drive a post just so
I have something to pose
a sweat-shaped glove on
in a gesture they think is their name.

*

The flute is the bone of something without organs; its sound is what breath unobstructed through you should compose.

\*

Twelve days they've trekked
moss back from the higher
parts in scraping cages
of goosevine, thread it
to trellis frames like broad beans
climb, to fashion little sails
yellowing at the edges
they slip around hollering
EXEUNT at the orders of
the eldest, a river throated
man, eyes small as salt.

\*

You hear the one about the pioneer who, chagrined, unwrapped his mail-order *bridge*?

*

Costumed primarily in pollens and pinecones,
they are indistinct to me,
interchangeable and muddled, misplacing my hearing,
except for one whose crotch protrudes its instrument from
    the faintest meringue I remember from childhood.

Standing prismatic on a sedan, she claims
to whoever's my wife and I,
who've attended the debut because we were going to eat
    cheese and crackers there anyway.

*

From the darkness around me
a voice asks *how large*
*is your mother's house* she
gazes from a shower
curtain she dices with a fish
knife, tells the number
of roses in the yard *she have*
*tits like yours* another
rises, answers the number
of daffodils, they finale by towing a balsa-wood replica
of my body through a pond they have fabricated
tied to her tongue, I cover my son's ears
at the applause, they should be to the next town in weeks.

\*

In the distance,

a seaplane lands
on rock. The horizon turns

· me on on
me me on.

*

Behold the discredited social studies teacher, our narrator, some months on at the store where everybody works, transformed by the accounted pageant—shaved head, white tank top tinged green, some tattoos we never saw when he was chalking around his antique globes—ordering dry roast beef sandwiches and an extra one with mayo for the skinny thing with him. He had a cane but a lot of people use them now: diabetes. You can't blame him. He filled an old orange juice jug with water at the tap outside. "49% of people think they are in the minority," one of his commencement speeches said.

*

He had a flat but didn't want our help: he said a friend was coming, then squinted, questioned if we had a cellular phone, and—Cokey did—called someone hunched in whatever shade could be beside his car. The backseat was covered with Gatorades and finished word searches. The car's roof was stained in a blur, like from mulch. A solo heaved on the tape deck. His sunburn kept some white from his fingers when he stood, uncrossed his arms, paused in massaging his own neck. He thanked us before we could look away.

\*

They said ignore him at the auditions for community theater, though the director had given him a clipboard and several frozen lemonades. In the bathroom he chipped at the whiteness between tiles, said it was for the squirrels. His lips had their styrofoam aspect. He said to himself, "Even if you haven't yet, don't." There was no year he was born in.

\*

From the top of the water tower that was really a gas tower we could see him. He let his dogs out and peed with them on his rock yard then peed on them a little, we believed singing. Tongue like a coming apart sponge in the urine steam, past dried birds hung on his chainlink like a hedge. The odor of scrambled eggs. Skin of his arms like his sleeves were rolled up, though he didn't have a shirt. When the light in the house behind him flashed again, I felt secure as a sprig in an empty jar.

*Nine*

Light early enough
to see
in the interior
courtyard
I woke momentarily roused
orange hibiscus
The human eye
achieves its eventual
mass
by age seven

People on this island say what
people on any island say
The sun takes
24 hours
to set
A wind-grey
fence
Reddest barbed wire
I have seen
And those flowers milk
on wheat
I couldn't get close
enough to know
if each was more than a single petal
Island horse: no
horse
stands so still or brown

In the mind there is a tiny open
hand for
anything you might
All the denim
arrived from the east, the blanks
grown easy: pony,
stone, same part
of each heel
worn
If you turn your head
the sky is
changed

Free of anything
except what
it's like now
there is no more need
to say
The grounds
of the coffee disperse
one way or another
She reads
pages uncut or
newly stuck

For a while Sancho
Panza
is played by a live duck
Every mechanic
has a guy
like this: yellow sideburns,
cigarette, he waits
for customers
where no one is
A kind of Midas: whatever
I grasp
goes dark
Trust in the seasons
does not allow
this fruit leaping
from a kicked stump

The only one who stays
as long as me
is a man flying around
on a dragon
Rainbow lodged
in the farthest stipulated
cloud
You shouldn't expect me
to have a name
This place assumes
a lost and found
Anything that pleases the eye
you'll come to caress

If one is plucked
three grow
The dress or
hands near where
the cello rests in celestial
The eye seen most when one
manipulates a contact
lens

The glass drinking jars
sun-hatched
on shelves was the word
*huckleberry*
or *honeysuckle*
Is there any feeling between panic
and numbness
Only the pairing of wine
There can be no meditation
now that you are about to look away

One knows from the smell
of the restaurant
downstairs if someone
has ordered now
catfish now the fiery prawns
I couldn't tell the plain
cave drawings
from the eyes I descended with
You can play the newest tune
on absolutely any instrument

If the definition of desire is
continual
It's always right,
the music: the afterlife
is a quiet, corporate place
Bad coffee is free, OK
coffee a nickel
I'm talking to somebody just
out of sight
or farther from it
than you realize if you see them

This sacred route was
made by pilgrims
marking each
step with a stone
A wall formed they walked
and dropped
their stones along
so this sacred route
moved gradually west

Before much
a pile of sandwiches
coffee with the ice
melted in it
My life moving
mostly in pauses
one's lightest
look refutes
We wait at
an earth berm pressing
an estuary's
complicated lattices
of salt beneath the sheen

# Acknowledgments

I'm grateful to the editors of the journals that first published this book's poems, often in earlier forms: *Interrupture*, *Iowa Review*, *jubilat*, *Matter Monthly*, *Modern Language Studies*, *notnostrums*, *Ossuary Whispers*, *Phoebe*, *Rumpus*, *Sprung Formal*, *Transom*, *Washington Square Review*, and *Witness*.

Jacob Cooper adapted a portion of the book for his musical composition "There is a way to say it that doesn't remember."

For essential support, I'm grateful to Kathy Savich, Hilary Plum, Caryl Pagel, Andy Stallings, Philadelphia's poets, Carrie Olivia Adams, Janaka Stucky, and my colleagues and students at the University of the Arts.